Chameleons

BY ELIZABETH RAUM

amicus high interest

Amicus High Interest is an imprint of Amicus
P.O. Box 227, Mankato, MN 56002
www.amicuspublishing.us

Library of Congress Cataloging-in-Publication Data
Raum, Elizabeth, author.
Chameleons / by Elizabeth Raum.
pages cm. — (Lizards)
Audience: Grades K to grade 3.
Summary: "Describes chameleons, including what they look like, where they live, why they change color, how they reproduce, and how they fit in the world"— Provided by publisher.
Includes bibliographical references and index.
ISBN 978-1-60753-484-6 (library binding) —
ISBN 978-1-62588-308-7 (pbk)
ISBN 978-1-60753-697-0 (ebook)
1. Chameleons—Juvenile literature. I. Title.
QL666.L23R38 2015
597.95'6–dc23

2013028237

Editor: Wendy Dieker
Series Designer: Kathleen Petelinsek
Book Designer: Heather Dreisbach
Photo Researcher: Kurtis Kinneman

Photo Credits: Cover, Superstock; all photos by Superstock except Alamy 23, 26; Shutterstock 10, 18–19, 21, 29

Table of Contents

Color Changers

A tan-colored chameleon clings to a tree branch. This is his **territory**. When another chameleon shows up, the first one reacts. In a flash, he goes from tan to bright green. It's a warning. It means, "Stay away!" Chameleons change color when they are scared, angry, too cold, or too warm. They can change colors to send messages.

Q What is the chameleon saying when he changes color?

This chameleon will change color to send messages.

A It could be lots of things! Males change color to show interest in females.

Leopard chameleons grow to about 17 inches (43 cm) long.

There are more than 150 different kinds, or **species**, of chameleons. They all change color. Most are between 7 and 10 inches (17.8 and 25.4 cm) long. Some are very tiny—only about 1 inch (2.5 cm) long. Others grow to 25 inches (63.5 cm). Their bodies are flat from side to side. Some even look like leaves or twigs. This helps them hide from enemies.

Looking at Chameleons

It might be hard to spot a chameleon. Chameleons blend in with the trees. This helps them hunt for food. Most chameleons spend their lives in trees. They are good climbers. But they move very slowly. A chameleon waits quietly on a tree branch. When an insect flies by, he'll be ready to grab it.

This chameleon's color helps it hide in the leaves.

A chameleon catches bugs with its superlong tongue.

Q What do chameleons eat?

Have you ever seen such a long tongue? A chameleon's tongue is as long as the chameleon! It's fast, too. The chameleon sees an insect. It shoots its tongue toward the bug. The chameleon's tongue has a sticky tip. The tongue wraps around the insect. The chameleon pulls the insect into its mouth.

A Chameleons eat insects, spiders, and scorpions. Bigger chameleons eat small birds.

The chameleon has big googly eyes. Each eye works separately. One may look up while the other looks to the side. This helps the chameleon know exactly where to aim its powerful tongue. Chameleons rarely miss their targets. They can snatch flying insects right out of the air.

A chameleon's googly eyes help it spot bugs to eat.

Life in the Trees

Chameleons live in the forests of Africa. Many live on the island of Madagascar, off the east coast of Africa. Some live in southeastern Asia and southern Spain. Most chameleons make their homes in trees. Their bodies are well suited to life in the trees. They are able to climb along thin tree branches.

Chameleons can climb thin branches.

Slowly, chameleons creep along. Their toes cling to branches.

Q How well do chameleons move on the ground?

No other lizards move like chameleons do. The chameleon wraps its toes around a branch. The toes act like our fingers. They grip the branch and pull the chameleon forward. Chameleons move one leg at a time. They move so slowly that it may be hard to tell that they are moving at all.

A Not very well. They are clumsy. They have nothing to hold onto.

Chameleons have **prehensile** tails. This means that the tail holds onto things. The tail helps the chameleon hang onto tree branches. When not in use, the tail curls up. Some lizards have tails that break off and regrow. Not chameleons. Chameleons need their tails every day in the trees.

The tail curls up to keep safe.

All chameleons have growths on their heads. Some have a crest. Other growths look like horns. But they are not really horns. They are called **casques**. Casques are soft and move easily, unlike horns. Casques collect water droplets. At night, water rolls down the casque into the chameleon's mouth.

Q Which chameleons have casques or crests?

Some chameleons have growths called casques.

A Generally, males are more likely to have them than females.

Finding a Mate

Male chameleons bob their heads and puff out their throats to attract females. The males may puff out their bodies or change colors. If the female is interested, she mates with the male. If not, she may run away or face the male and hiss. If he doesn't get the message, the female may attack or even bite. Her bite hurts!

A male and female come together to mate.

After mating, the female goes off to lay eggs. The female digs a pit or tunnel for the eggs. She may bury them under rocks or leaves. Smaller species lay 2 to 4 eggs. Larger species lay up to 100 eggs. The babies hatch in about 3 months. They never know their parents. But they know how to survive on their own.

Babies hatch and take care of themselves.

Snakes will eat small chameleons.

A Place in the World

Chameleons have many enemies. Snakes, birds, and monkeys eat them. Chameleons are safest in trees. Their color and shape protect them. Humans can be a more dangerous enemy. Pet dealers capture chameleons and sell them as pets. Pet chameleons require special care and handling. Many die once they leave the forest.

The biggest problem chameleons face is losing their **habitat**, or home. Madagascar is home to many species of chameleons. It is the world's fifth largest island. People in Madagascar are clearing many forests. They use the wood for fires. Without the trees, chameleons have no place to live.

Chameleons need these trees to live in.

Glossary

casque A helmet-shaped or horn-shaped growth on a chameleon's head.

habitat The natural environment or home for a particular animal.

prehensile Able to grasp or take a hold of something.

species A kind or group of animals that share certain characteristics.

territory Land or water that belongs to a particular animal.

Read More

Rabe, Tish. *Miles and Miles of Reptiles.* New York: Random House, 2009.

Sirota, Lyn A. *Chameleons.* Mankato, Minn.: Capstone Press, 2010.

Stewart, Melissa. *How Do Chameleons Change Color?* New York: Marshall Cavendish, 2009.

Websites

Baby Chameleons: National Geographic
http://video.nationalgeographic.com/video/kids/animals-pets-kids/reptiles-kids/chameleon-babies-kids/

Chameleon: Natural History Museum
http://www.nhm.ac.uk/kids-only/life/life-disguise/chameleon/index.html

Chameleons: National Wildlife Federation
http://www.nwf.org/Kids/Ranger-Rick/Animals/Amphibians-and-Reptiles/Chameleons.aspx

Every effort has been made to ensure that these websites are appropriate for children. However, because of the nature of the Internet, it is impossible to guarantee that these sites will remain active indefinitely or that their contents will not be altered.

Index

About the Author

Elizabeth Raum has worked as a teacher, librarian, and writer. She has written dozens of books for young readers. She likes doing research and learning about new topics, and especially enjoyed learning about lizards. Even so, she doesn't want one for a pet! Dogs and cats are cuddlier. Visit her website at www.elizabethraum.net.